Contents

KU-754-476

Unsolved mysteries

For centuries, people have been puzzled and fascinated by mysterious places, creatures and events. Is there really a monster in Loch Ness? Did the lost city of Atlantis ever exist? Are crop circles messages from **aliens** or clever hoaxes? Are UFOs visiting alien spacecraft or simply tricks of the light? Is there alien life on Mars or Venus?

Some of these mysteries have baffled scientists, who have spent years trying to find the answer. But just how far can science go? Can it really explain the unexplained? Are there some mysteries which science simply cannot solve? Read on, and try to make up your own mind ...

This book tells you about the search for alien life. It looks at eyewitness accounts of alien life, at the methods that **astronomers** and other scientists are using to try to find signs of **extra-terrestrial** life, and at what successes they have had so far.

Hundreds of movie and TV programme makers have tried to guess what aliens would look like.

Are we alone?

When you watch **science fiction** films or television programmes, or read a science fiction book, do you ever wonder whether the aliens shown in them could really exist? You might ask the same question when you look up at the night sky. Are there other animals and plants out there in space? Or is the Earth the only place in the **Universe** where life exists? In short, are we alone?

Finding out about life on other planets is not just a matter of curiosity. It might help us to understand the Universe and how it works, how life on Earth started in the first place, how the human race developed, and what might happen to it in the distant future.

Are there other planets like Earth among the billions of stars?

On one hand, alien life seems very unlikely. Some scientists think that we might be the only intelligent life in our **galaxy**, or even in the Universe. On the other hand, why should the Earth be unique? Other scientists think that there simply must be other intelligent life in the Universe.

This book looks at two main questions: Is there (or was there) life elsewhere in our **Solar System**? And are there planets outside our Solar System where life could exist? What can science do to answer these questions?

Beginnings of a mystery

Nobody knows when people first started to wonder whether there is other life in the **Universe**. Until a few hundred years ago, most people believed that the Earth was at the centre of the Universe. They did not know what the stars were, or about the other planets in the **Solar System**, which they thought were 'wandering' stars.

The invention of the telescope in the 17th century allowed **astronomers** to see that these wandering stars were actually solid planets that reflected light from the Sun rather than making light themselves. The first scientist to say it was possible that life existed on other planets was the Dutch astronomer, Christtiaan Huygens (1629–95). At the time, there was no reason to believe that it didn't.

One of Percival Lowell's (see right) sketches of Martian canals.

Martian 'canals'

Only a hundred years ago, many top scientists still thought it was perfectly possible that there was life on our neighbouring planet, Mars. This was due largely to the Italian astronomer, Giovanni Schiaparelli (1835–1910), who examined the surface of Mars through telescopes and described the long, straight channels he saw. The Italian word for channels is *canali*, which was wrongly translated as 'canals'.

Soon everybody was talking about Martians! Among them was the American astronomer, Percival Lowell (1855–1916). He spent years studying the 'canals'. He believed that they had been built by intelligent beings to carry water to dry areas of the planet to water crops. When space probes finally visited Mars in the 1960s, they found no trace of these canals. They can only have been some sort of **optical illusion**.

A popular science fiction magazine from 1948. Interest in UFOs and flying saucers grew in the 1940s and 50s.

The Guzman Prize

In Paris in 1900, a prize of 100,000 French francs (a huge amount of money at the time) was offered to the first person to communicate with **extra-terrestrials**. Contact with Martians was excluded, because people were convinced that there was life on Mars, and that contacting them would be too easy!

Seeing the aliens

The easiest way of solving our mystery would be to actually see **aliens** from other planets! So has anybody ever seen alien life?

The only **extra-terrestrial** place that people have visited is the Moon. The astronauts who landed there in the 1960s and 70s did not see any signs of life, but most **astronomers** accepted that the Moon was a dead world long before this. The only other places we have seen are the surfaces of Mars and Venus, which have been photographed by space probes that have landed. Their cameras saw no life either.

One sighting of a life-form that scientists think could be alien is in the form of a fossil in a lump of rock. The rock is a **meteorite** that originated on Mars. The fossil could be of a tiny **micro-organism**.

Several Apollo missions to the Moon by US astronauts proved it to be a lifeless world.

8

Alien sightings on Earth

Every year there are hundreds of sightings of unidentified flying objects (UFOs) in the sky. Most of these are caused by the weather, or are actually aircraft. But some are unexplained. Many people believe that these are alien spacecraft spying on us. Some people say they have met aliens on Earth, and some even claim that they have been whisked away by aliens for a few hours. Here are two typical eyewitness accounts of aliens.

Goose Bay, Labrador, Canada, 1954

US military pilot Kenneth Arnold was the first person to use the phrase 'flying saucer' to describe the UFO he saw in 1947.

Three hours into a flight from New York to London, the captain of a Stratocruiser airliner saw seven UFOs in a formation. The airliner's crew and several passengers described the UFOs as globes – six small and one large. They kept pace with the airliner for 20 minutes, occasionally changing formation, but when a military jet was sent to investigate them, they disappeared.

Kelly Hopkinsville, Kentucky, USA, 1955

On a summer evening, Billy Ray Taylor was staying with friends on their farm and went out to get water from the well. He saw a UFO, which he described as very bright with a multi-coloured exhaust. His friends assumed he had seen a shooting star. But an hour later, several short creatures with glowing bodies and huge heads and ears approached the house. The owners shot at them, but the bullets did no harm. In the morning there was no trace of the creatures.

Planets, moons and stars

Before we can think about whether **alien** life could exist in the **Universe**, we need to understand a bit about the size and structure of the Universe, and about how stars and planets like our Sun and the Earth are formed.

Solar systems

The Earth is one member of a family of planets that **orbit** the Sun, which is our local star. The Sun, the planets and the moons that orbit the planets, are known as the **Solar System**. The Solar System formed out of an enormous cloud of gas and dust. Gravity pulled the gas and dust together to form the Sun. Left-over material formed the planets and moons.

A solar system is a family of planets orbiting a star.

The life of a star

In the centre of a star there are **nuclear reactions** happening that create huge amounts **energy**. The star gives out this energy as heat, light and other forms of **radiation**.

The Sun is a pretty average sort of star. It started shining about 5000 million years ago, and will shine for another 5000 million years. Before it dies, it will expand, probably swallowing up the inner planets, including the Earth.

Making the Earth

Our Solar System contains some small planets with rocky surfaces, such as the Earth and Mars, and some large planets with liquid surfaces, called the gas giants, such as Jupiter and Saturn. The Earth formed about 4600 million years ago. It started life as a ball of molten rock. For 1000 million years, it was bombarded by lumps of rock floating about in space. It was also covered in volcanoes. Oceans and the **atmosphere** formed about 3500 million years ago.

Unmanned spacecraft can visit planets in our Solar System. This photo of the surface of Mercury was taken by Mariner 10 in 1974.

The size of the Universe

All the stars you can see in the night sky are members of a huge group of stars called the Milky Way. The Milky Way is a **galaxy**. It contains roughly 400 billion stars, and is about 100,000 **light years** across (a light year is the distance that light travels in a year – about 9.5 million million kilometres). More staggering still is that the Universe contains about 100 billion galaxies! And there's no reason why many of the stars in these galaxies should not have solar systems of their own.

What is life?

What do you think of when you hear the word 'life'? You probably think of humans and the thousands of other species of animals, trees and flowers. But remember that most **organisms** on Earth are **micro-organisms**, such as **bacteria**, that you can only see through a **microscope**. The easiest definition of life is an organism that grows and reproduces itself.

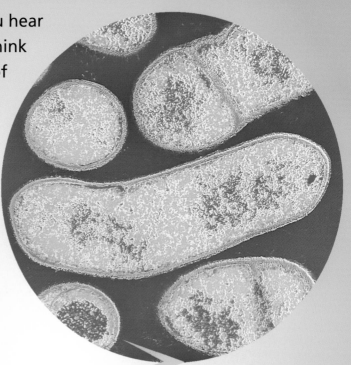

Conditions for life

Animals, plants and other organisms must have certain things in order to grow and live. The most important requirements are water in liquid form (rather than ice or steam) and a source of **energy**. Animals get energy from the food they eat, and plants get energy from sunlight. Life likes warm, wet places best, as you can see from the abundant life in rainforests. It cannot flourish where there is no water, or where it is freezing cold or boiling hot.

Bacteria can be found in all environments on Earth. Is it possible that these tiny organisms could be found on other planets?

What makes a planet suitable for life?

Life can only exist on planets where conditions are suitable. This means that a planet must be close enough to its star for water to remain liquid, but not so close that it boils away.

Astronomers call this region the 'habitable zone'. The Earth is inside the habitable zone of the Sun. For life to exist on the surface, a planet must also have an **atmosphere** that cuts out harmful rays from the Sun.

Life in strange places

In recent years, micro-organisms have been found in some pretty nasty places. For example, green **algae** have been found living under rocks in dry, cold Arctic regions, inside rocks in dry, hot deserts, and in piping hot water next to **geysers**. Perhaps most amazingly, micro-organisms have been found living next to thermal vents several kilometres under the sea. There is no light here, so the organisms get **energy** from the water, which is so hot that on the surface it would be boiling.

Micro-organisms can also survive dormant for thousands of years, even in space. Apollo 12 astronauts found bacteria on a camera that had been left there two years earlier! These findings tell us that life can exist in places where scientists previously thought that it could not survive.

Some bacteria can even survive near volcanic vents, many kilometres below the surface of the oceans.

Life from soup

We know that the Earth was formed about 4600 million years ago. It started its life as a huge ball of molten rock where life could not exist. And we know that now there are millions of different species of animals and plants that inhabit almost the whole surface of the Earth, including intelligent life, such as humans, great apes and dolphins. So where did life on Earth come from? What did the first forms of life look like? And how did we develop from them?

Palaeontologists study the fossilized remains of animals and plants to try to understand how life evolved.

Why we need to know

If we can find out and understand how life began on Earth, and what the conditions on Earth were like when it started, we will be able to understand how life could start (or could have already started) on other planets, and look for planets where the conditions are the same today.

Scientists from several different branches of science are involved in trying to find out how and when life started on Earth. They include **geologists**, **climatologists**, **palaeontologists** and **biochemists**.

The theory so far

At the moment, we still don't actually know how life
started, but there is a theory about it. Millions of years after
the Earth was formed, oceans began to form from water in
the **atmosphere**. Huge electric storms raged all the time,
and **meteorites** were crashing into the surface. Under these
conditions, it is thought that simple chemicals were made
to react together to form more complex chemicals in
the oceans.

The oceans full of chemicals are known as the primeval
soup. Somehow, more than 3500 million years ago, these
complex chemicals reacted together to form extremely
simple **organisms** that could recreate themselves. The latest
theory is that this happened near **hydrothermal vents** under
the sea, quite by accident.

These organisms were our **ancestors**! Life remained very
simple for another two billion years before simple plants
such as **algae** developed, then more complex plants and
simple animals. Over hundred of millions of years
the different species we know today evolved.

If it's true that life started **spontaneously** on
Earth from a mixture of chemicals, then
there's no reason to think that the same
thing could not happen in similar conditions
elsewhere in the Universe.

*A meteorite crater
in Arizona, USA. The
enormous energy of an impact
could have caused chemical
reactions in the primeval
soup.*

Life in our Solar System

The easiest place for us to look for **alien** life is in our own **Solar System**. Even with the most powerful telescopes we cannot see the surfaces of the other planets and moons to see if there is any life there. But we can investigate the conditions on them by examining them with special telescopes, and by sending probes. So we can get an idea of whether they could support life.

Even the chances of life on the Moon could not be ruled out until astronauts landed there in 1969. The astronauts went into quarantine when they arrived back on Earth, just in case they were carrying microscopic life back with them!

Spacecraft send back data about the atmospheres and surfaces of planets and moons. This information gives scientists a better idea about whether they could support life.

Our habitable zone

Remember that **astronomers** call the region around a star where life could exist on planets the **habitable zone**. Jupiter, Saturn, Uranus, Neptune and Pluto are outside the habitable zone of our Sun. Mercury, Venus, Earth and Mars are inside it. Mercury has no **atmosphere**, and has huge temperature swings from night to day. Venus has a thick atmosphere containing sulphuric acid, and the temperature on the surface is more than 450 °C. So life on these two planets is impossible. But it might have existed billions of years ago.

16

How do we know about planets?

Astronomers use special telescopes, such as infra-red telescopes, to investigate the surfaces or atmospheres of the planets and their moons. They can find out what temperature the surface is and what chemicals are in the atmosphere. Space probes have **orbited** and landed on most of the planets and several moons. They have taken photographs, used **radar** to make maps, and measured the chemical composition of their atmospheres and surface rocks.

Life on Europa?

Although Jupiter is outside the habitable zone, the Galileo probe that flew close to its moon, Europa, in 1989 seemed to show that there is an ocean of liquid water underneath its icy surface. Could conditions in the water be right for life?

Is there life lurking under the icy surface of Jupiter's moon Europa?

Life on Mars

Although our neighbouring planet, Mars, is only half the size of the Earth, it is similar to Earth in several ways. Its day is about the same length, it has a thin **atmosphere**, and it has polar **ice-caps** that look like the Earth's ice-caps. Mars seems the most likely place to find **extra-terrestrial** life in our **Solar System**. On the next four pages you can find out how **astronomers** and other scientists are trying to find life there.

Probes to Mars

The first space probe to visit Mars was *Mariner 4* in 1965. It took photographs of a small section of the planet's surface. To the dismay of the **NASA** mission scientists, the photographs showed a cratered surface like the surface of the Moon, with no signs of life. Two more probes in 1969 showed the same features in different places.

At first glance the Martian surface looks lifeless.

In 1971 another probe, *Mariner 9*, arrived to map the whole surface of Mars. Scientists were amazed to see pictures of huge volcanoes, including one 25 kilometres high, and deep chasms, like dry river beds, hundreds of kilometres wide. They concluded that these chasms must have been eroded by vast quantities of flowing water, and immediately thought of the possibility of life. They planned a mission to land on the surface and test for life.

A Viking *lander* scooping up Martian soil to test it for simple life.

Viking tests for life

The *Viking* probes landed on Mars in 1976. They collected Martian soil with a scoop and carried out experiments to test for **micro-organisms**. In two experiments, a sample of soil was dropped into a liquid containing food. If there were micro-organisms in the soil, they would digest the food, making waste gases such as oxygen and carbon dioxide in the process. The two experiments tested for these gases. A third experiment tested for **photosynthesis** happening, which would show that there were simple plants, such as **algae**, in the soil.

NASA scientists were delighted and amazed when all three of these experiments gave positive results. That was until the results of another experiment showed that there were no **organic chemicals** in the soil, which meant that life could not exist there. The scientists realized that the positive tests were the result of other chemicals in the Martian soil. For the time being, hope for life on Mars was shattered.

Fresh hopes for Martian life

Today, there is fresh hope of finding life on Mars. There are several reasons for this. The discovery of green **algae** living inside rocks in very cold, very dry Arctic regions of the Earth has demonstrated that **micro-organisms** can live in the sort of conditions found on the surface of Mars. Future probes to Mars will look inside rocks. Rocks might also contain fossils of **organisms** that lived on Mars millions of years ago, when conditions were more like those on Earth.

In 1999, the Mars Global Surveyor took photographs that showed evidence of liquid water deep under the surface of the planet. This shows that there must have been oceans on Mars in the past. Perhaps there are still creatures living in the underground water.

Are these tube-like structures fossilized remains of micro-organisms? Scientists believe that the meteorite they were found in may have come from Mars.

The Martian meteorite

In 1996, hope for life on Mars was given a boost by the discovery of what may be a fossil of a Martian micro-organism. It was found inside a **meteorite** called ALH84001, which was discovered in Antarctica in 1984. Experts think the meteorite came from Mars, because it contained little pockets of gas that matched the gas in the Martian **atmosphere**. They think it was formed when a monster meteor hit Mars, throwing molten rock out into space.

Inside the meteorite are what look like fossils of micro-organisms. They resemble tiny worms. The discovery caused a sensation around the world. Evidence of life on Mars had finally been found! Or had it?

Did we arrive by accident?

The fact that meteorite ALH84001, and several other meteorites, were discovered to have come from Mars shows that pieces of one planet can end up falling on another, even though the planets are millions of kilometres apart. Some scientists think it's possible that life on Earth did not start on its own, but was brought from Mars on a meteorite. So we may all be descended from Martian micro-organisms!

Investigations cannot show if it is actually is a fossil, so there is no proof. The subject is still under debate.

This is what a huge meteorite crashing into Earth might have looked like.

The search for other planets

We've looked at the possibility of life on other planets in our **Solar System**, but what about planets outside it? We know that there are countless billions of stars in the **Universe**, many of them similar to our Sun. It seems likely that there should be planets (called extra-solar planets) **orbiting** these stars too. The first step in the search for life outside the Solar System is to find other Earth-like planets.

Too small to see

The big problem with finding extra-solar planets is that they are so far away! The nearest star to the Sun is 4 **light years** away. At that distance, spotting an Earth-sized planet is like spotting a football on Mars! Another problem is that any light reflected from a planet would be swamped by the light from its star.

The Hubble Space Telescope has taken photographs that seem to show planets around distant stars.

Spot the wobble

At the moment, the only way to tell whether there are planets orbiting another star is to use powerful telescopes to look for the effects that planets have on a star. There are two main effects. The first is that as planets orbit a star, their gravity makes the star wobble very slightly from side to side. We can just spot these wobbles from Earth, but only if the planets are very big. The second effect is that as a planet passes between the star and the Earth, it blocks out a tiny bit of the light from the star. This makes the star twinkle very slightly.

The search continues

The first proof of a planet outside the Solar System came in 1995. Since then, **astronomers** have found evidence of planets around several other stars. For example, a planet half the size of Jupiter is orbiting a star called 51 Pegasi, which is 60 light years from Earth. A planet three times as big as Jupiter is orbiting a star 50 light years away, called 47 Ursae Majoris, in the Big Dipper.

The problem is that many of these planets are closer to their stars than Mercury is to our Sun, showing that their solar systems are very different to our own, and are unlikely to have Earth-like planets. But the search for rocky planets like Earth continues. There are plans for a huge telescope, called the Terrestrial Planet Finder, that would go into space to look for them.

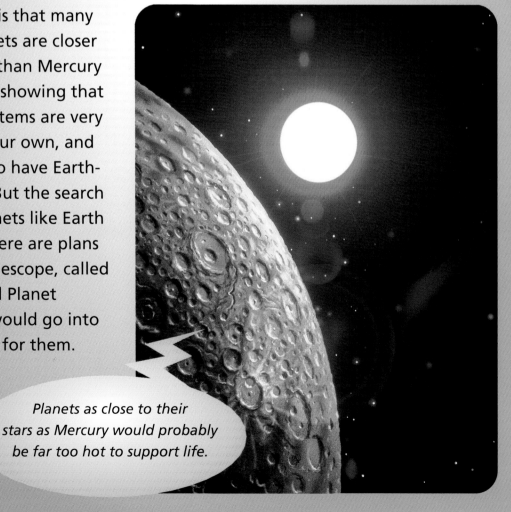

Planets as close to their stars as Mercury would probably be far too hot to support life.

Waiting for signals

Even if we do detect Earth-like planets in other solar systems, how can we prove that there is life on them? Using current space technology, sending probes would be impractical. They would take a hundred thousand years to reach even our nearest star.

Signals from other planets

Some scientists think that the best way to look for life outside the **Solar System** is to look for signs of advanced technology. This assumes that intelligent life has evolved on other planets, and that it has developed technology at least as advanced as ours. There might, for example, be radio signals coming from other planets. These could have been sent deliberately by other intelligent life searching for us, or could simply be signals that have escaped into space, in the same way that signals from our communications systems are going into space all the time. Because these signals travel at the speed of light, they would take only a few years to arrive on Earth.

The search is on

The first attempt to detect signals from other worlds was called project Ozma. The Ozma scientists aimed a **radio telescope** at two nearby stars similar to the Sun. They listened for 150 hours but found no signals.

The current search is called the Search for Extra-Terrestrial Intelligence (SETI). The SETI Institute was formed in 1984. It was originally paid for by **NASA**, but is now privately financed. Its Project Phoenix is searching for signals from **alien** life, using several huge radio telescopes around the world. They try to find radio signals coming from space that seem to have some sort of message in them. The telescopes are being aimed at stars within 150 **light years** of Earth, where we know there is a chance of Earth-like planets being found.

Unfortunately, the telescopes also pick up messages that have come from communication systems on Earth. SETI uses two telescopes at once to try to filter out these confusing messages. Then computers search through any signals to try to find meaningful messages. So far no extra-terrestrial signals have been spotted.

An array of radio telescopes can detect extremely weak signals from space.

Fakes and frights

It would be very difficult to go to another planet, make some fake **alien** life and have it discovered by scientists! So it's no surprise that nobody has ever claimed to have found aliens on another planet. However, plenty of people have faked photographs of alien spacecraft and creatures on Earth.

George Adamski, 1952

One of the most famous alien encounters involved 61-year-old George Adamski. It was the first report of a human meeting an alien. Adamski claimed that he had gone into the Californian desert to watch for UFOs. He had seen one – a flying saucer 11 metres across – and close by was a figure, which he described as human-like, of average height, with tanned skin, long gold hair and green eyes. Adamski talked to the alien in sign language and by telepathy, and discovered that it came from Venus.

Later, Adamski claimed that he had met more aliens, and that they had taken him to meet other aliens on Venus, Mars and other planets. At the time many people believed Adamski, but we now know that there is no life on the planets he mentioned. It's likely that he made everything up.

A reconstruction of an alien supposedly found at Roswell, New Mexico. Many people believe that aliens have visited Earth but we can never be sure.

Why make fakes?

Why do people like Adamski try to fake sightings of spacecraft and aliens? One obvious reason is to try to make money by selling the story to a newspaper, or by writing a book. In fact, Adamski published several best-selling books about aliens, including one called *Flying Saucers Have Landed*. Other people fake UFO photos just for fun, or to impress their friends.

Fact or fiction?

The report of visiting aliens that had most effect on people was not a fake, but fiction. In 1898, H.G. Wells published a novel about a Martian invasion of Earth, called War of the Worlds. *Orson Welles made* War of the Worlds *into a radio play that was broadcast in America in 1938. An actor played the part of a radio reporter watching the Martians attacking Earth in their tripod spacecraft, and killing people with heat rays. The first episode caused panic among millions of radio listeners, who thought the reports were real! They rang family and friends to tell them to leave New York, where the Martians were supposed to be heading.*

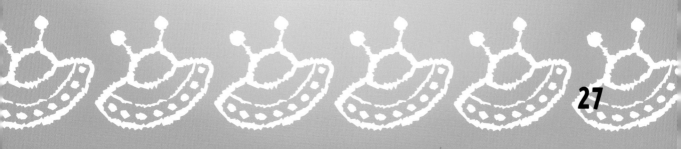

In conclusion

So can science really solve the mystery of life on other planets? To prove that alien life existed, scientists would need hard evidence, such as film of an **alien** or living **bacteria** from another planet. At the moment, we have no proof of the existence of alien life, either inside our **Solar System** or on planets in other solar systems.

One of the billions of galaxies in the Universe. Surely there must be life somewhere here.

What is certain is that in the last three decades we have made huge advances in the search for **extra-terrestrial** life. We've found that there are water and other chemicals needed for life on other planets and moons in the Solar System. And we've possibly discovered a fossil of an ancient Martian life form. We've also found that there are planets round other stars in our **galaxy**.

But the mystery of life on other planets is not something we are going to solve quickly. It may take many decades and dozens of space missions before we can find proof of other life in the Solar System. And it may take far longer to find Earth-like planets outside our Solar System and hundreds or even thousands of years to find out if there is life on them.

Most **astronomers** think it's quite possible, and even quite likely that there is life out there in the **Universe**. After all, we only understand a tiny fraction of the things that happen in the Universe, so we cannot assume we are special or unique. But astronomers will not believe it until there is real proof.

What do you think?

Now you have read about the scientific investigations into extra-terrestrial life, can you draw any conclusions? Do you think that there must be other planets like Earth in the vastness of the Universe, with animals and plants living on them? Or do you think that chances of life starting elsewhere are just too small? Do you have any theories of your own about where life came from?

Perhaps you believe that some UFOs are alien visitors? Or do you think that aliens would have contacted us if they had reached the Earth? Perhaps you think that looking for alien life is a waste of time and money because it may take millions of years to get an answer.

Try to keep an open mind. Bear in mind that if scientists throughout history had not bothered to investigate things that appeared to be strange or mysterious, many scientific discoveries may never have been made.

Are there creatures on other planets exploring the space around them as we are?

29

Glossary

algae group of plants that lives in water and damp places. Some algae are made up of a single plant cell.

alien living creature that does not come from the Earth

ancestor person that another person is descended from, or an animal that humans have evolved from

astronomer person who studies space and the objects in space

atmosphere blanket of gases around a planet. Only some planets have an atmosphere.

bacteria microscopically small organisms that are made up of a single cell. They are not animals or plants.

biochemist person who studies biochemistry, which is the science of the chemistry that happens inside living things

climatologist person who studies the world's climates and how they are changing

energy power or ability of something to make something else work, e.g. electricity and heat.

extra-terrestrial describes any object or being which does not come from the Earth

galaxy huge group of stars in space. Galaxies can contain billions of stars. Our own galaxy is called the Milky Way.

geologist person who studies the Earth, the history of the Earth and the rocks that make up the Earth

geyser hole in the ground from which hot water and steam, heated by hot rocks underground, regularly shoot upwards

habitable zone area around a star where the conditions for life can exist on planets

hydrothermal vent hole on the sea bed, thousands of metres below the surface, from which hot, mineral rich water escapes

ice-cap thick covering of ice at the north or south pole of a planet

light year distance light travels in a year, equivalent to 9.5 million million kilometres

meteorite piece of rock from space which hurtles through the Earth's atmosphere and hits the ground, where it makes a crater

microscope device that makes a very small object look much larger. There are optical microscopes and electron microscopes.

micro-organism organism that is too small to see with the naked eye, such as a bacteria

NASA National Aeronautics and Space Administration in the United States of America

nuclear reaction splitting of the nucleus of an atom, or the joining together of two nuclei of two atoms

optical illusion image seen by the eye that is not what it seems. For example, a flick book shows a series of still pictures which appear animated.

orbit path that an object, such as a moon or a satellite, takes as it moves around a star or a planet

organic chemicals chemicals that are found in living things, or that come from living things

organism anything that is living

palaeontologist person who studies palaeontology, which is the science of fossils

photosynthesis process by which plants make food using the energy in sunlight

radar device which can detect objects in the air. It sends out radio waves and detects any which bounce off objects and return. The objects are shown on the radar's screen.

radiation waves, rays or streams of particles

radio telescope instrument that detects radio waves coming from objects in space. It has a dish-shaped aerial that collects the radio waves.

science fiction fictional stories about space or the future

Solar System the Sun and its family of planets and moons

spontaneously instantly

Universe everything that exists

Index

Titles in the *Can Science Solve* series include:

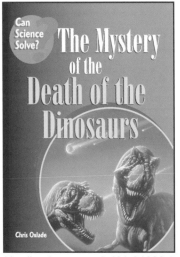

Hardback   0 431 01623 2

Hardback   0 431 02040 X

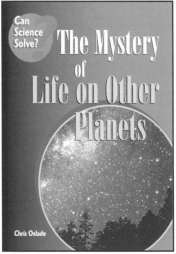

Hardback   0 431 01624 0

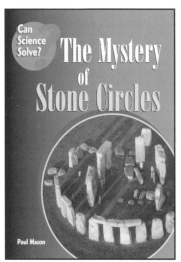

Hardback   0 431 01625 9

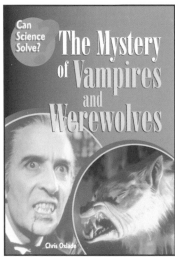

Hardback   0 431 01622 4

Find out about the other titles in this series on our website www.heinemann.co.uk/library